Summer Heat

by Frederick Prugh
illustrated by Kristen Goeters

Core Decodable 71

Bothell, WA • Chicago, IL • Columbus, OH • New York, NY

MHEonline.com

Copyright © 2015 McGraw-Hill Education

All rights reserved. No part of this publication may be reproduced or distributed in any form or by any means, or stored in a database or retrieval system, without the prior written consent of McGraw-Hill Education, including, but not limited to, network storage or transmission, or broadcast for distance learning.

Send all inquiries to:
McGraw-Hill Education
8787 Orion Place
Columbus, OH 43240

ISBN: 978-0-02-132109-4
MHID: 0-02-132109-4

Printed in the United States of America.

2 3 4 5 6 7 8 9 DOC 20 19 18 17 16 15

It will be a hot two weeks.
Jean and Dean feel the heat.

"Time for the beach you two?" asks Mom.
"Yes!" yell Jean and Dean.

Cars fill the streets.
They drive east to the beach.

Jean and Dean reach the beach.
The two kids see and smell the sea.

Jean sticks her two feet in the sea.
Dean feels the sea breeze.

"Mom, the beach is neat," Jean calls.
"I agree," adds Dean.